> *"A soulmate is someone to whom we feel profoundly connected as though the communication and communing that take place between us were not the product of intentional efforts but rather a divine grace."*
>
> —Thomas Moore

ARE YOU READY TO EXPERIENCE unimaginable love and manifest a soulmate who will appreciate and adore you? A life partner who will cherish you and be devoted to you?

I didn't meet and marry my soulmate until I was forty-four, and I've learned a lot along the way about what does and doesn't work in the world of love and romance. To manifest my soulmate I used everything I had ever learned about the Law of Attraction, psychology, and spirituality. My intentions became crystal clear while I simultaneously cleared out the clutter in my house *and* in my heart. I learned and invented techniques, rituals, visualizations, and prayers that helped me prepare my body, mind, spirit, and home for an amazing relationship. And they worked. I met my husband, Brian, within months of beginning this process. He has exceeded all of my desires and expectations. He was, and is, everything I ever wished for.

It's not your job to know *how* your soulmate is going to appear; you simply need to be ready, willing, and open to love. The Law of Attraction states that you will attract to you those things that match your state of being. The Universe mirrors back to us our beliefs about ourselves and the world. Believing that your soulmate is out there is critical to the preparation of manifestation. Finding true love is possible for anyone, at any age, if you are willing to prepare yourself on all levels to become a magnet for love.

Inkspirations Love by Design is a transformational coloring book that provides you with a complete and proven process to manifest your soulmate—one that has worked for tens of thousands of people worldwide. The visual delight of these spectacular images by artist Manja Burton adds to the process by bringing your creative passion to the pages. By following the instructions, step-by-step, and mindfully coloring the drawings with whatever resonates in your heart, I know that you, too, will be reunited with your true love.

Wishing you love and magical kisses,
Arielle Ford

PS: Please visit *www.soulmatesecret.com/color* to watch an instructional video on optimizing the Law of Attraction and this coloring book to manifest the love of your life.

> "Love is the spirit that
> motivates the artist's journey."
>
> —Eric Maisel

Transform Yourself with the Art of Love

THE LAW OF ATTRACTION works by preparing you, in mind, body, and spirit, to manifest your deepest dreams and desires. What you think about comes about, and what you focus on blossoms and grows in your life.

Coloring can help accelerate this process by taking you to a place that is free from outside distraction. By taking gel pen, marker, or pencil to paper, you are reaching your core self and entering the realm of endless possibility. Taking time out for peace and solitude each day is essential to your well-being. It is nourishment for the mind and soul and, when done along with Arielle Ford's exercises, will help you to set an intention for manifesting the love of your life.

The drawings in this book offer a wide variety of styles and types. From intricate patterns in mindful mandalas, to flowing fields of flowers, and simple frames to accentuate your written thoughts and intentions, all are designed to enhance the exercises that will ready your mind and heart to receive love.

About the Author

ARIELLE FORD is a love and relationship expert and a leading personality in the personal growth and contemporary spirituality movement. For the past 25 years she has been living, teaching, and promoting consciousness through all forms of media. She is a speaker, a blogger for the *Huffington Post,* and the producer and host of Evolving Wisdom's *Art of Love* series. Arielle is a gifted writer and the author of 10 books, including the international bestseller *The Soulmate Secret: Manifest the Love of Your Life with the Law of Attraction* and *Turn Your Mate into Your Soulmate.* She has been called "The Cupid of Consciousness" and "The Fairy Godmother of Love." She lives with her husband and soulmate, Brian Hilliard, and their feline friends. *www.arielleford.com*

About the Illustrator

MANJA BURTON is a freelance artist and illustrator who is the founder of the popular website *Hattifant: Toys & Décor That Inspire Mindful Play & Nurture Imagination*. She has volunteered globally for Envision, UNICEF, and Save the Children. She also worked with Turquoise Mountain, an organization in Kabul, Afghanistan, founded at the request of HRH Prince Charles of Wales and former president Hamid Karzai, designed to revive Afghanistan's traditional crafts and to regenerate Murad Khani, an historic area known for its rich cultural heritage. *www.hattifant.com*

A Note from the Illustrator

AS AN ARTIST, I believe that creativity opens our minds and hearts to all of life's possibilities. I was especially honored to illustrate *Inkspirations Love by Design*, knowing that my art would help bring couples together by illustrating Arielle Ford's time-honored principles. My husband—my soulmate—and I have had the opportunity to travel and live in vastly different cultures around the globe. This has informed my work, which has both Eastern and Western influences; it is sometimes free-flowing and other times balanced and symmetrical. I subscribe to the philosophy that the path in life that we follow forms us, and we create the path in front of us. As you color my drawings, focus on the present moment and think deeply about the love that exists for you—that which you simply need to uncover. Follow the lead of your heart as you choose colors. Experiment with blending and take chances with patterns and textures. Add touches of glitter if you want sparkle in your drawings. Don't think or criticize, simply feel, and the right decisions will come to you—both in your artwork and in your life.

—*Manja Burton*

Coloring Tools and Tips

COLORED PENCILS: With a variety of shapes and sizes, colored pencils are great for shading or blending colors together, both of which add interest and depth to any design.

GEL PENS AND MARKERS: Magic markers and gel pens are good for adding bold, defined bursts of color.

CRAYONS: A staple of any household with kids, crayons are surprisingly versatile when filling in large spaces.

TIP: Add a piece of scrap paper under each page you're working on to make sure that the color doesn't bleed through the page.

Choose Your Colors

You can use both complementary and analogous colors to make a gorgeous piece of art—the possibilities are as endless as your imagination.

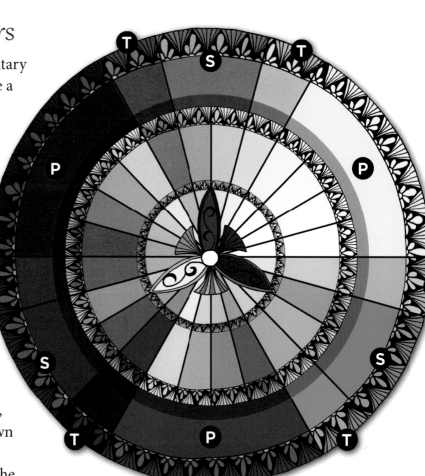

PRIMARY COLORS
The primary colors—red, yellow, and blue—are denoted by a "P" on the outside of the color wheel. Primary colors cannot be created by mixing any other colors.

SECONDARY COLORS
The secondary colors—green, orange, and purple—are shown by an "S" on the color wheel. These are formed by mixing the primary colors.

TERTIARY COLORS
Yellow-orange, red-orange, red-purple, blue-purple, blue-green, and yellow-green make up the tertiary colors, which are noted with a "T" on the outside of the wheel. These colors are formed by mixing a primary color with a secondary color.

Inspiration Is All Around You

NOT SURE WHAT COLORS TO USE? You can find a rainbow of inspiration all around you in your daily life. Remember that hearts don't always need to be pink and red—they can still be just as romantic in blue and green, or even yellow and silver. It's all up to you! Take a few minutes to look and to really notice the patterns of different plants and animals, the colors of the flowers that dot your street, and the radiant hues of the sunset or the morning sky. By being more mindful of the colors that make up your day, you can make them come alive in your own creations. Get inspired by the designs on the following pages. As you will see, each artist lends his or her own style and personality to the artwork. Some pieces are colored bright and bold, others use soft and sweet pastels. Some artists choose to fill every space with color, while others use the white space to let their artwork breathe. Each piece is as unique as the person who colored it.

A nature-inspired color scheme with analogous colors

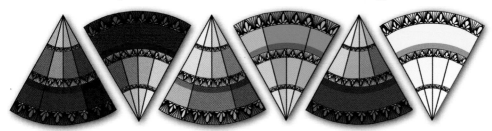

ANALOGOUS COLORS are any three colors which are side by side on a 12-part color wheel, such as yellow-green, yellow, and yellow-orange or teal blue, blue, and indigo.

A nature-inspired color scheme with complementary colors

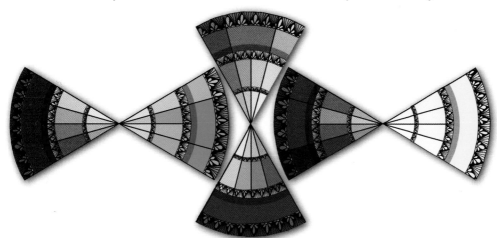

COMPLEMENTARY COLORS are any two colors that are directly opposite each other, such as yellow and purple or orange and blue.

Marker art by Manja Burton.

Colored pencil art by Dawn Grove.

Marker and glitter art by Eleanor Kosow.

Colored pencil art by Christine Belleris.

Colored pencil art by Kevin Stawieray.

Colored pencil art by Kevin Stawieray.

Colored pencil art by Dawn Grove.

Gel pen art by Kim Weiss.

I see life with my soulmate as

Intention

Live in the knowingness that you deserve to have a loving, committed relationship by affirming your clear intention that the One you have asked for is already yours. You are connected, on unseen planes, and it is up to you to set the stage for your physical connection. Step into your truth; speak your deepest desire to manifest your soulmate by writing your vision of yourself, in relationship with your beloved, as clearly as you can on the following page.

Marker art by Eleanor Kosow.

my life with my soulmate as

Belief

When deep down at the core of your being you believe your soulmate exists, there is no limit to the way he or she can appear. Allow for the signs or symbols—a song on the radio, the beauty of the sunset—to gently remind you that your soulmate is on the way!

Trust

*"In a soulmate relationship one plus one
does not equal two, it equals eleven,
and your love blesses the world."*

—Brian Hilliard, my husband and soulmate

Trust that there is enough love in the world to fill your heart with love—and then some.

Today, on a separate sheet of paper or in the white space of the drawing on the following page, make a list of the soulmates you *already* have in your life. These are the people—even pets—who love you just the way you are. By focusing on the love you already have, trust that you become a magnet for more love!

Surrender

When the seeds of a flower have been planted and the first leaves begin to sprout, the gardener doesn't tug on the leaves every day to make the plant grow faster.

While gardeners know they need to nurture their plants to make them grow more beautiful, they also can't force nature. This is the same with love. You've practiced setting your intention, belief, and trust that your soulmate is out there and you will be together, but today you need to surrender to divine timing and to destiny. Simply prepare yourself in body, mind, and soul and then relax into the knowledge that the One you've asked for is on the way.

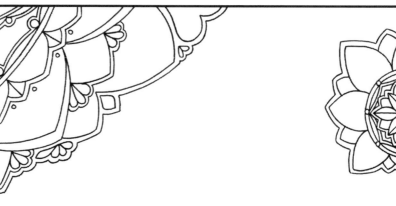

Clarity

Having "crystal clarity" about the heart traits and qualities you most desire in a soulmate is critical in order to manifest your beloved. It's up to you to carefully place your order with the universe. What are your "must-haves" and your "deal breakers?" Write them in the yin-yang mandala on the following page or on a separate sheet of paper.

Forgiveness

Before we can accept new love into our lives, we have to release any hurt and upset we are still holding on to from the past. It is a willingness to let go of the hurt and suffering, the anger and blame against others or ourselves because of something that happened yesterday. We don't need to forget, but we do need to let go. Forgiveness allows us to heal and be more at peace in the present moment.

Today, on a separate piece of paper, write a letter (that you will never send) to the one you need to forgive. End it with, "I forgive you, I bless you, and I set you free." Then, write a second letter from them to you. You actually channel them and have them tell you the story of what happened from their perspective, which usually results in finding out that they never really meant to cause harm. Again, end it with, "I forgive you, I bless you, and I set you free."

(You can then destroy the letters by shredding, burning, or simply throwing them away.)

I forgive you,
I bless you,
I set you free!

Soulmate Wish List

A "soulmate wish list" identifies the heart traits and qualities that will support your long-term happiness. The number one item on your soulmate wish list should be as specific as possible, almost like a classified ad posted in the universe—a call for someone who is open, willing, and available to you right now. For example: "My soulmate is straight/gay, open, willing and available for a long-term, monogamous marriage/partnership, with/without children."

The second item on your wish list should be around the area of geography. If you live in San Francisco, and you know that you want to spend the rest of your life there, number two on your soulmate wish list would be, "My soulmate lives in San Francisco or is willing to move."

If you don't care where you live, if geography is not an issue, you can leave this off.

Releasing Your
Soulmate Wish List

Now that you have written out and designed your soulmate wish list, you need to release it to the universe. Detach the list on the previous page, read it again, and send it off with a deep prayer of gratitude. I took mine to the ocean, burned it, and scattered the ashes into the water. Then I took myself to lunch and toasted my soulmate with a glass of champagne. In my mind I said to him, *The cosmic welcome mat is now out. Whenever you're ready, I am ready for you.*

You can release your list any way that resonates with you—putting it inside your pillowcase, under your mattress, or copying and reducing it down to fit into a balloon that you can send into the sky . . .

Coloring the Love Mandala

As you color in each section of the beautiful love mandala on the next page, concentrate on the traits or qualities about your soulmate that you envision or desire. You can also voice them out loud, as my friend Gayle did, who said as she colored: "I would like a man who is kind to animals," and, "My soulmate loves my sense of humor," and even "My soulmate has a cute butt." Within weeks, she met her soulmate—who had all these qualities! They have now been married for more than thirty years.

Releasing Limiting Beliefs or Thoughts

Every time you move through an issue that has kept your heart closed, you liberate suppressed energy and free up valuable space in your life. There's an art to managing your thoughts and emotions so that even when doubt, fear, or other limiting feelings pop up, you are not swept into a spiral of negativity. This requires the mental discipline to focus your attention on what you *desire* rather than on what you *don't* want. If I catch myself dwelling in a negative or unpleasant thought or feeling, I say to myself *cancel-cancel*, and I then intentionally create a new vision for myself. Sometimes, this simple shift in perception is all I need to stay aligned with my desired outcome.

The process of attracting your soulmate can get discouraging at times. But if you're approaching it from the mindset of "It's been a year and it still hasn't happened," you're living in the reality of what's missing. The Universe simply can't add more love to your life when you're focused on the love you don't have. On the next page, take a minute to write out all the ways you have love in your life right now.

Love Now!

You were born to be loved, cherished, and adored. We are all already connected to each other through the divine matrix. This means that you can begin the relationship right now, today! I call this, "love before first sight." One way to begin this process of connecting to your soulmate, on the unseen dimension, is to have a daily internal conversation with them. Share the details of your life with them. Tell them about all the fun things you will do when you are together in the 3-D, physical world. Begin building the connection. It really works!

Make Plans

Live as if your soulmate *is already* a part of your life. When you do this, you send out an irresistible signal that you are ready *now!* When you're *living as if,* your behavior follows your belief, and if your belief is, "The one that I've asked for is on the way," then what does that behavior look like?

A fun way to "live as if" is to begin making plans for the future. This could be buying them greeting cards for birthdays, anniversaries, and Valentine's Day. You could buy tickets to concerts or plays. When you are invited to a big event, RSVP "plus one." Wake up every day in joyful anticipation that your beloved is on the way.

Ready for Romance!

Beautify yourself and your space as if preparing for a very romantic evening with your beloved. Imagine you are about to host a king or queen for dinner. What do you need to do to prepare for their arrival? It could be as simple as adding new throw pillows in the living room, candles and fresh flowers on the dining room table, and creating a delicious dinner menu. This is another way to strongly practice *living as if.*

Growing Your Self-Love

You will attract someone who energetically matches the degree of esteem you have for yourself. Just as seeds grow in the warmth of the sun, so do our positive qualities when we put our attention upon them. For instance, if your wish is to be with someone who is affectionate, devoted, and kind, then make a commitment to bring forth those qualities within yourself.

A great way to think of this assignment is to imagine that you *are* the man or woman of your dreams. Next, ask yourself, "If I were my beloved, would I fall in love with me? And if the answer is "no," then dedicate yourself to becoming someone you *would* fall in love with.

Today, look for opportunities where you can demonstrate devotion, kindness, and affection to others and the world around you. And then, most importantly, can you give those things to yourself? When you fall in love with yourself, the world mirrors that love back to you. Speaking of mirrors, every time you walk past a mirror, be sure to blow yourself a kiss! Or post positive messages there to yourself on sticky notes.

Out with the Old!

Toss out the old to make room for the new. Do you have "A," "B," and "C" clothes? "A's" being your favorite clothes, the things you feel really great in. "C" clothes are the ones you are saving for the day you plan to paint your house. And "B" clothes are somewhere in the middle. What if you got *rid* of all of your "B" and "C" clothes and *only wear* "A" clothes so that you always look good and, most importantly, *feel* your best?

Indulge

Indulge all of your senses with flowers, clothes, tasty delights, and sexy items!

What you put your attention on grows. When we focus on self-love and indulging ourselves, we attract more love. What would "spoiling" yourself look like for you?

Here are some suggestions:

- Write yourself a love letter on the following page. Give yourself the freedom to express all the things you most love and appreciate about yourself.

- Gaze into a mirror, look deep into your own eyes, and speak these words out loud:

    "I really love you. You are a totally wonderful, beautiful, magical person deserving of great love."

- Buy yourself a special gift, perhaps a piece of jewelry you can wear daily as a reminder of how much you admire yourself!

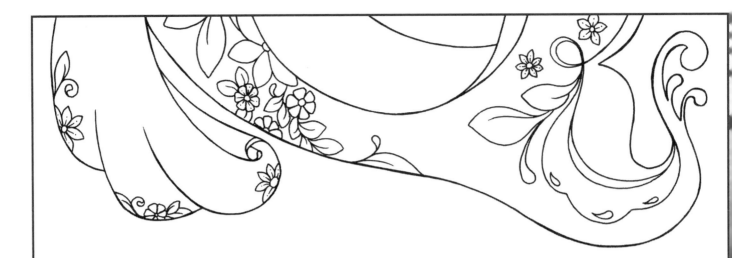

Flirt!

An important part of practicing the Law of Attraction comes from the word "attraction," which contains the word "action." One of the fastest and easiest ways to be "in action" is to consciously practice flirting every day. Flirting is a playful way to engage someone in conversation, and it can be done in a friendly, not necessarily sexual manner. Think of it as networking for your romantic life!

Before you try this out on someone to whom you are super attracted, I suggest spending a week practicing by complimenting three strangers a day (men, women, and children). Make eye contact and smile. Try a simple compliment such as, "I love the color of your shirt, it really makes your eyes pop," or, "Wow, great watch, I really like the style." Be friendly, open, and don't have any expectations. The point is just to open a door and see what happens.

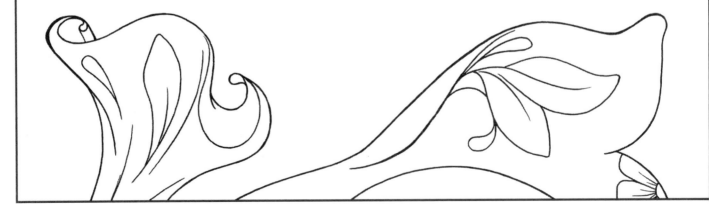

Feathering the Nest

It's time to prepare your home for the arrival of your beloved. The first step is to clear the clutter of all the piles of magazines, the "junk drawers," the stacks of unused items that you step over every day. Get rid of it and create fresh, clean space in your home. Letting go of the old makes room for the new and it allows the energies to flow effortlessly.

The next step is to carefully look around your home at the photographs, souvenirs, and mementos on display. If any of these are connected to an ex-partner, throw them away, give them away, or at the very least put them in a box in the garage or attic. Every time you look at one of these items you are subconsciously reconnecting with your past instead of looking toward the future. If you have children living at home and some of the photos include your ex-partner, create a special place in the hallway to their bedroom or in their bedroom for those photos to exist but definitely do not have them in the more public spaces of your home.

Cutting Cords: Releasing the Past

Old lovers leave energetic cords in you and on you, tying you to the past. These cords can energetically block you from bringing in somebody new. To be completely free of our energetic connections to past lovers, you need to cut these cords. Stand up and, using your imagination, see the other person standing in front of you a few feet away with a cord of energy connecting you to them, belly button to belly button. Next, take your hand and make a karate chop motion three times to cut the cord. Afterward, clap your hands three times and then wash your hands.

If you've cut the cord with somebody really significant, it's possible you might hear from them because, on some level, they're going to feel that this energetic cord has been cut. If they contact you, keep the conversation really short then cut cords again. Just because they called, and they may have said they miss you, it doesn't mean they're coming back. It means they miss the connection; they miss that energy.

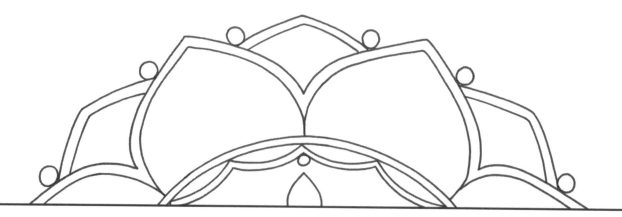

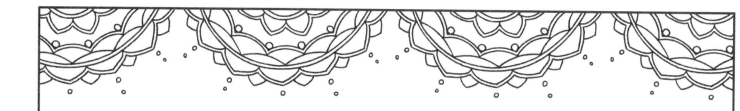

Make Space

If you make the space for it, love will find its way to you. When making your home ready to receive your soulmate, it's really important to make room in your home for them and their stuff.

Begin in the bedroom. Make sure that there's a nightstand on their side of the bed, that it's the same height as yours, and is totally empty. Make sure that there's at least one empty drawer in the dresser. And clear at least half of a shelf in the bathroom cabinet. Also, be sure to give them six or seven inches in the closet. Nature abhors a vacuum, so the fastest way to get their clothes into your closet is to make space for them. If you can't tolerate some empty space in your closet, then buy them a new bathrobe and leave the tag still on it and hang it in "their space." You might even want to move your car to one side of the garage. This way, they're going to feel welcome knowing that you've anticipated their arrival.

Full Moon Ritual

Use the power of the goddesses and the full moon to generate love. Begin by taking a *love bath* an hour or two before the moonrise. Surround your tub with pink or red candles and some roses. Add a little rose oil, and if you wish you can also add a few drops of: ylang ylang (to balance your male and female energies); sandalwood (great for attracting love); and jasmine (said to be a favorite of Cleopatra's and very seductive). Soak in the tub while focusing your attention on your heart and imagining the joy and fulfillment of being in the arms of your soulmate.

Then, go to the most romantic place in nature you can get to—a place that you want to someday take your soulmate to—or just go outside in your back yard. Plan to be there just before the moonrise time. Bring a crystal, charm, or piece of jewelry to hold in your hand to charge with these full-moon energies. Also, bring a blanket or pillow to sit on (ideally pink or red), a favorite celebratory beverage, and a champagne flute. You will also need a journal, a container of sea salt, and a bell (if you have one). Place your blanket or pillow on the ground and make a wide circle around it with the salt. Sit down and imagine your energies connecting deeply with the earth.

Write in your journal what you are most grateful for about the life you now lead, and what you are grateful for that is soon to come with the arrival of your soulmate. Then, close your eyes and say a prayer of gratitude and meditate for a while. When you are ready, open your eyes and gaze at the moon, drawing its energy and light into your body, mind, spirit, and heart. When you are done, pour your drink and raise a toast to your soulmate and tell him or her (in your mind) that the cosmic welcome mat is now out and you look forward to meeting them on the physical plane in the near future. If you brought a bell, now is the time to ring it!

Treasure Map

Create a visual representation of the love life you
are manifesting by making a treasure map or vision board. You'll need
to set aside an hour or two for the project and these materials:

- One good-sized piece of poster board or foam board

- A glue stick and a pair of scissors

- A stack of your favorite magazines that reflect your unique
  interests, as well as general lifestyle, women's, décor, or wedding
  publications

Cut out the images, words, and photographs that most appeal to you
and collage them onto the poster board. They should represent love,
romance, commitment, family, and joy. Make sure that one of these
photos is of a loving couple. It could be something as simple as two
people walking on a beach hand in hand. When choosing
these images, find those with the *feeling* you want to evoke
as opposed to manifesting the models. If marriage is what
you desire, then you may want to add wedding rings, a
wedding cake, etc. Be sure to include a photo of yourself
where you're looking really happy, and then surround that
image with words that express your positive beliefs about
finding love. Affirm that you already are loved, cherished,
and adored by your perfect partner.

Create a Sacred Altar

Create a sacred love altar to place in the marriage and relationship corner of either your home or your bedroom. To find the best spot, first stand in the front door, facing into your house or apartment; the far right corner of your home is your marriage and relationship corner. Then stand in the doorway of your bedroom and notice the far right corner of that room, which is also your relationship corner. You can energize one or both of these.

One of the ways that you energize or "raise the chi" in this area is to hang a pink quartz crystal, or a quartz crystal on a pink or red ribbon, from the ceiling. It can be spherical, round, or heart-shaped. Be sure to have pictures or statues of animal couples: swans, cranes, dolphins, or doves. All of these species mate for life. Add two red, pink, or peach-colored candles. I always like to put a plant in my relationship corner that is nice and lush with heart-shaped leaves. You can also hang a wind chime there. Finally, add fresh flowers. (Please note, according to Feng Shui principles, do not have any dead, dry flowers anywhere in your home.)

The sacred love altar will provide a really beautiful visual addition to your home or your bedroom, and serve as a focal point to help you clarify and magnetize what you want in a relationship. You can also put your treasure map above your altar, which is what I did. This is a place where you can sit and meditate and talk to your soulmate.

Be a Pleasure Pig

Prepare your heart, mind, and soul for love by building your oxytocin levels. When you want to feel more love, you can do it by consciously releasing the hormone oxytocin into your brain. Known as the "bonding" hormone or the "superglue of love," oxytocin is really good for you.

One of the things that depletes our levels of oxytocin is stress. Who doesn't have an overload of that? A simple twenty-second hug, gazing into the eyes of someone you love, or petting your dog or cat will also boost your oxytocin levels. Here are several other oxytocin rebuilders:

- Getting your hair done
- Having a manicure and pedicure
- Shopping (you don't have to buy anything just looking and touching work)
- Getting a massage
- Going to live concerts and soaking up the music through every sense
- Slowly eating and savoring every bite of a favorite treat
- Laughing
- Taking a nice, long bubble bath with candles
- Dancing

Prayer

Daily prayers of gratitude and giving thanks for your amazing life, in present moment awareness, works wonders. Try this Daily Soulmate Manifestation Prayer:

> God, Goddess, and all that is, in this moment I am grateful for the healing of my heart of everything that would stop me from attracting my soulmate. In this moment, I remember that my perfect, right partner is magnetizing to me, and my only job is to rest in perfect awareness that their heart is already joined with mine as I savor the waiting, and so it is.

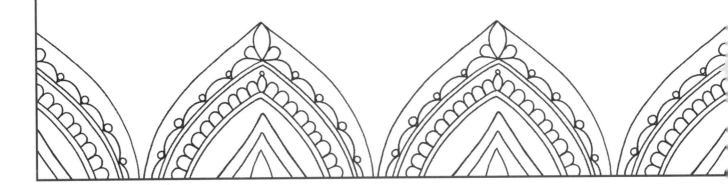

Guidance

Your ancestors, angels and guides on the "other side" are ready, willing, and available to assist you. Just ask them to send you someone!

After you have colored the angel on the next page, you can make a copy—or wait until you have finished the whole book—cut her out, and hang her in your window as a reminder that loving guidance is all around you.

Turn on Your Heart Light

Find a place where you can sit quietly for at least five minutes. Close your eyes and take five slow, deep breaths. Relax into the chair, with your feet flat on the ground, and let your shoulders drop while you release the tension in your body. Begin to shift your attention away from your mind and focus on the area around your heart. Now, imagine a time when you felt love. Fully feel and re-experience this love as if it were happening right now.

Keeping your attention on the area around your heart, imagine that you are inside of it, and you have located your own personal "heart light." Turn the light on and up to its brightest setting. Imagine the rays of light broadcasting your purest feelings of love and appreciation out into the world. Know that you are beaming a signal to the heart of your soulmate with the message that you are ready and willing to magnetize him or her into your world. Sink into the knowingness that you have now touched your soulmate by the energy of your heart. Breathe into the deep knowingness that he or she is on the way. Know that it is safe to keep your heart light on. Remember that you have much love to give and much love to receive. When you are ready, open your eyes, keeping your heart open as you do.

———————

For a free audio experience of this feelingization, please visit www.soulmatesecret.com *and click on the tab "free stuff."*

Affirm

When it comes to manifesting a soulmate, the single most important thing on which to have total clarity is how you desire to *feel* when you are with your beloved. For now, let go of your physical "wish list" and move into the "feeling space." Close your eyes and imagine you are lying in bed next to your soulmate. How are you feeling? Loved? Happy? Safe? Serene? Excited? Relieved? Filled with gratitude? Experience the depth of your positive emotions for your love connection.

In your mind, whisper words of love, appreciation, and gratitude to your soulmate. Tell them that you now know and trust they are on the way to you. Affirm that you are happy, satisfied, and content. Experience the fullness of you as the giver and receiver of love. Feel yourself as lover and beloved.

Take a Risk

Dating is an essential part of the soulmate manifestation process. While many believe that that they can size up a person in thirty seconds, research shows that it takes most women five dates before they truly discover whether or not they are attracted to a man. So while you shouldn't ignore really negative vibes, don't necessarily let your first impression stop you from what could be a situation where you potentially pass up the man or woman of your dreams.

Today, take a big, bold, brave step in the dating world. Set up an online dating profile, or call a few friends and ask them to set you up on a date. Join a group or club that interests you, or simply change up your routine and go to a new coffee shop or a new place for lunch. Your soulmate is looking for you, and you must become available and visible to make love happen.

Be a Love Philanthropist

*"The only thing that can be lacking
in any situation is that which
you are not giving"*

—A Course in Miracles

If you believe that you have enough fresh air to breathe and enough clean water to drink, then each day take time to remember that there is more than enough love in the world for you. Make a daily, conscious effort to freely give your love to those around you. By doing this, you automatically become a magnet for more love coming your way.

Learn Wabi Sabi Love!

Wabi Sabi is an ancient Japanese art form that honors all things old, weathered, worn, imperfect, and impermanent by finding the beauty in the imperfections. For instance, if you had a large vase with a big crack down the middle of it, a Japanese art museum would put the vase on a pedestal and shine a light on the crack. Or, they might fill the crack with 24 karat gold!

Wabi Sabi Love is devoted to exploring the simple, fun, and effective ways to apply this concept to our love relationships and demonstrate how to attain groundbreaking shifts in perception. By doing so, you can embrace and find the beauty and perfection in yourself and in each other's imperfections. I call this "going from annoyed to enjoyed!"

Letter from the Future

Today, we remember and re-experience the day we met our beloved. "The Letter from the Future" is a process that projects you into the future to feel, see, and remind you that you are already connected to your soulmate. You write this letter AS IF it has already happened.

Here are the directions: Imagine that you have now been in a totally loving, happy, committed relationship with your soulmate for at least six months. Put a date at the top of the following page. It can be nine months from now or one year from now; just pick a date far enough in the future that you will have already spent six months with your soulmate.

Now write a letter, and share all the details about how happy you are, and how good it feels to finally be sharing your life with your beloved. Include details about what he or she is like, and things that you have done and will be doing together, including your future plans. Write in as much detail as possible and really share the depth of your emotion. Then, if you wish, you can email me the letter at *arielleford@gmail.com.* Be sure to place a copy of this letter on top of or underneath your sacred love altar if you have one.

*"Where there is great love, there
are always miracles."*

—Willa Cather

The pathway to lifelong love is easier when you've got the right tools.
At *arielleford.com,* you will join a community of people who are dedicated to
fulfilling their romantic destinies. There, you will find success stories and blog
posts to inspire you, and information on Arielle Ford's books, classes, speaking
engagements, and products that will help you along your journey.

If you enjoyed this coloring book, then I'd like to ask you for a favor:

Would you be kind enough to leave a review on *www.amazon.com,
www.bn.com,* or *www.bamm.com?* It'd be greatly appreciated!

—Arielle

Coloring is a fun, creative, and powerful way to enrich our lives. If you like
Inkspirations Love by Design, be sure to check out HCI's full line of coloring
books for adults, including:

Inkspirations Mindful Living

Inkspirations Create While You Wait

Inkspirations in the Garden

Inkspirations for a Happy Heart

Inkspirations for Women

Inkspirations Animal Kingdom

Inkspirations for Cat Lovers

Inkspirations for Dog Lovers